FOOTBALL
THE MATH OF THE GAME

BY SHANE FREDERICK

CAPSTONE PRESS
a capstone imprint

Sports Illustrated KIDS Sports Math is published by Capstone Press,
1710 Roe Crest Drive, North Mankato, Minnesota 56003.
www.capstonepub.com

Books published by Capstone Press are manufactured with paper
containing at least 10 percent post-consumer waste.

Library of Congress Cataloging-in-Publication Data
Frederick, Shane.
    Football : the math of the game / by Shane Frederick.
        p. cm.—(Sports illustrated kids sports math)
    Includes bibliographical references and index.
    Summary: "Presents the mathematical concepts involved with the sport of football"—Provided
by publisher.
    ISBN 978-1-4296-6567-4 (library binding)
    ISBN 978-1-4296-7319-8 (paperback)
    1. Football—Mathematical models—Juvenile literature. I. Title. II. Series.
    GV950.7.F735 2012
    796.332—dc22   2011007864

Editorial Credits
Anthony Wacholtz, editor; Alison Thiele, designer; Eric Gohl, media researcher;
    Eric Manske, production specialist

Photo Credits
Shutterstock/Adam Derewecki, cover (back); Debra Hughes, design element;
    Petr Vaclavek, design element; Tony Campbell, 9 (bottom); Walter G
    Arce, 8 (bottom)
Sports Illustrated/Al Tielemans, 4–5, 24, 29 (top), 31 (bottom), 39 (bottom), 41 (all);
    Bill Frakes, 8–9, 23, 26; Bob Rosato, 16 (top), 21 (bottom), 25 (bottom), 36, 39
    (top); Damian Strohmeyer, 12, 19 (bottom), 21 (top), 22, 28 (top), 33 (all), 34,
    40 (top), 43, 44; David E. Klutho, 14; John Biever, 17, 19 (top), 35, 40 (bottom);
    John Iacono, 30; John W. McDonough, 29 (bottom), 37, 38, 45; Peter Read Miller,
    1, 10–11 (all), 13, 15, 16 (bottom), 25 (top), 32; Robert Beck, 18, 27, 42; Simon
    Bruty, cover (front), 6–7, 20, 28 (bottom), 31 (top)

Printed in the United States of America in Stevens Point, Wisconsin.
072013   007513R

TABLE OF CONTENTS

FOOTBALL AND MATH

What skills do you need to play football? Sure, you need to be big, strong, fast, and physical. But did you know you need to be good at math too?

Believe it or not, math is a big part of one of the roughest, toughest sports around. From measuring yards and compiling statistics to calculating probability and figuring out angles, there are a lot of numbers hidden inside football. Knowing what those numbers mean helps coaches call better plays, allows quarterbacks to make better passes, and makes defensive players better tacklers.

CHAPTER 1

Let's start where the action happens—on the football field. A National Football League field is 120 yards long. That includes 100 yards between the goal lines and two 10-yard end zones, one on either end. The field is 53 ⅓ yards wide. A yard is three feet, so how many feet long and wide is a football field?

$$120 \text{ yards} * 3 \text{ feet/yard} = 360 \text{ feet}$$
$$53 \tfrac{1}{3} \text{ yards} * 3 \text{ feet/yard} = 160 \text{ feet}$$

The field is big enough to hold 22 players (11 on each side) and seven game officials. All of them are moving around the turf once the ball is snapped for each play. How much room is there on the field?

To measure the total area of a football field, multiply its length by its width.

$$\text{area} = \text{length} * \text{width}$$
$$\text{area} = 360 \text{ feet} * 160 \text{ feet}$$
$$\text{area} = 57{,}600 \text{ square feet}$$

Let's plug in the original measurements to figure out what the area is in square yards.

$$\text{area} = 120 \text{ yards} * 53 \tfrac{1}{3} \text{ yards}$$

$$\text{area} = 6{,}400 \text{ square yards}$$

Because there are three feet in a yard, the amount of square feet should be three times the amount of square yards, right? Wrong! The amount of square feet is nine times greater than the amount of square yards. Although there are three feet in a yard, there are nine square feet in one square yard. Each of the amounts are squared.

$$1^2 = 1$$
$$3^2 = 9$$

Let's check the math.

$$\frac{57{,}600 \text{ square feet}}{6{,}400 \text{ square yards}} = \frac{9 \text{ square feet}}{\text{square yard}}$$

CANADIAN FOOTBALL LEAGUE

In the Canadian Football League, the field is 150 yards long, including 110 yards between the goal lines and two 20-yard end zones. It's also 65 yards wide. How much more area is there on a CFL field than an NFL field?

Answer: 3,350 square yards. CFL: 150 yards * 65 yards = 9,750 square yards – 6,400 square yards = 3,350 square yards

DOWN AND DISTANCE

To move the ball to the end zone or into scoring position, a team has to keep the chains moving. That means it has four plays, called downs, to gain 10 yards. Otherwise it must give up the ball to the other team. If it gets 10 yards, a new set of downs is awarded. If a team gets to fourth down and is out of field-goal range, it can choose to give it one more try or punt the ball to the other team.

Teams use addition and subtraction to determine what kind of plays they should try. If it's second down and one yard to go for a first down, the team might hand the ball to its running back and try to get that single yard. If it's third down and 15 yards to go, they'll likely pass the ball farther down the field in order to keep the chains moving.

DOWN MARKER

Offenses can move backward too. Defenses can push back runners or sack the quarterback, causing their opponents to lose yards. If it's second down and seven yards to go from the 25-yard line and the quarterback is sacked at the 19, what is the next down and distance? It's a 6-yard loss, so it will be third and 13.

THROW A FLAG

Football has plenty of rules to follow. If those rules are broken, a team is punished. The severity depends on the penalty. Here are some examples:

5 yards—defensive holding, delay of game, offsides, encroachment, false start, illegal formation, illegal motion

10 yards—offensive pass interference, offensive holding, illegal block, tripping

15 yards—roughing the passer, roughing the kicker, unnecessary roughness, unsportsmanlike conduct, facemask

For some penalties, such as defensive pass interference, the ball is moved to the place where the penalty occurred. Some defensive penalties also come with an automatic first down for the offense.

FLAG

TIME OF POSSESSION

One of the best ways to win a football game is to keep the offense on the field. The amount of time a team has the ball is called the time of possession (TOP). The minutes and seconds are displayed with a colon. For example, a TOP of 32 minutes and 5 seconds is shown as 32:05. Both teams' TOP add up to 60 minutes—the length of an NFL game.

On September 19, 2010, the St. Louis Rams squared off against the Oakland Raiders. The Raiders controlled the clock for 36:49. To figure out what percentage of the game the Raiders had the ball, convert 36:49 to seconds.

$$TOP = (36 * 60) + 49$$
$$TOP = 2,160 + 49$$
$$TOP = 2,209 \text{ seconds}$$

Finally divide the Raiders' TOP by the length of an NFL game.

$$60 \text{ minutes} * 60 \text{ seconds/minute} = 3,600 \text{ seconds}$$

$$2,209 / 3,600 = 61.4\%$$

The Raiders had control of the ball for more than 60 percent of the game. Despite a late Rams' touchdown, the Raiders won the game 16-14.

The team with the higher TOP doesn't always win the game. In a 2009 game between the Miami Dolphins and the Indianapolis Colts, the Dolphins controlled the ball for 45:07. Miami had the ball for 75.2 percent of the game. But the Colts used the little time they had wisely. They relied on passing and scored a late touchdown to win 27–23.

In 2010 the San Diego Chargers led the league in average TOP with 33:02. The Tennessee Titans were on the bottom of the list with a 26:01 average TOP.

THE PLAYOFFS

In the NFL the ultimate goal is to win the Super Bowl. But in order to do that, a team must first make the playoffs following a grinding 16-game regular season. There are 32 teams in the NFL, and 12 teams advance to postseason play. What percentage of the teams makes it to the postseason? Divide the number of playoff teams by the total number of teams.

$$12 / 32 = 0.375$$

That means 37.5 percent of the teams—a little more than one-third—make it into the playoffs.

The league is divided into two conferences—the AFC and the NFC. Each conference has four divisions, each with four teams. Each division champion gets a playoff spot. Each team has a 25 percent chance of winning their division ($1 / 4 = 0.25$). But there are also two wild card teams that advance from each conference. With the wild card teams, six out of 16 teams (37.5 percent) from each conference make the playoffs.

RAVENS VS. CHIEFS

In 2010 the Seattle Seahawks became the first team with a losing record to win its division and make the playoffs during a full season. The Seahawks won the NFC West with a 7–9 record. A pair of 10-win teams—the New York Giants and the Tampa Bay Buccaneers—missed out because they didn't win their divisions and there were better wild card teams.

SEAHAWKS VS. SAINTS

Once the playoff schedule is set, what chance does a team have of winning it all? There are 12 teams in the playoffs, so they have a 1 in 12 chance (1 / 12 = 0.083, or 8.3 percent). However, the two teams with the best records in each conference get byes to the second round. Because they have one less game to play, they enter the playoffs with a better chance of winning the Super Bowl (1 / 8 = 0.125, or 12.5 percent).

SUPER BOWL MATH

The New Orleans Saints took on the Indianapolis Colts for the NFL championship in 2010. They played in Super Bowl XLIV. The letters after the words "Super Bowl" are Roman numerals—numbers used in ancient Rome. The first Super Bowl is known as Super Bowl I, and the second is Super Bowl II. The Saints-Colts game was the 44th Super Bowl.

ROMAN NUMERALS	
I	1
V	5
X	10
L	50
C	100
D	500
M	1,000

Roman numerals can be tricky. Counting by ones, it goes I (1), II (2), III (3). But as you approach five, it changes. The Roman numeral for 4 is IV. The I (1) goes before the V (5) to show subtraction. The number 40 is treated the same way—the X (10) is before the L (50).

What will the Roman numeral be for the 52nd Super Bowl? The 68th?

ANSWER: LII (52) and LXVIII (68)

CHAPTER 2

OFFENSE

WHAT'S THE POINT?

The object of the game is to move the football as far into the opponent's territory as possible and score points. Get the ball across the goal line for a touchdown. Come up short and try to kick it through the uprights for a field goal.

The team with the most points at the end of the game is the winner. It's simple math. But it can get a little complicated. Teams use math to determine their strategy during games.

If a team is trailing by four points in the final minute of the game, a field goal isn't good enough. They need to score a touchdown.

POINTS	
Touchdown	6 points
Field Goal	3 points
Safety	2 points
PAT (point after touchdown) kick	1 point
PAT run/catch (2-point conversion)	2 points

ATLANTA FALCONS VS. ST. LOUIS RAMS

Let's take a closer look at an NFL game from November 21, 2010, when the Atlanta Falcons matched up against the St. Louis Rams. The Rams jumped ahead early, and the teams switched leads throughout the first three quarters. But in the fourth quarter, the Falcons extended their lead for a big win. From the scoring information, we can figure out the Falcons' final score.

FALCONS' SCORING RECAP

Field Goal: Bryant (3 points)
Touchdown pass from Ryan to Finneran (6 points) PAT: Bryant (1 point)
Field Goal: Bryant (3 points)
Field Goal: Bryant (3 points)
Touchdown pass from Ryan to Peelle (6 points) PAT: Bryant (1 point)
Field Goal: Bryant (3 points)
Rushing touchdown by Michael Turner (6 points) PAT pass from Ryan to White (2 points)

At the end of the game, the Falcons had 34 points.

NEW ORLEANS SAINTS VS. SAN FRANCISCO 49ERS

The following week, in a game between the New Orleans Saints and the San Francisco 49ers, the first points on the board came from a safety. The Saints had more scoring drives, but the 49ers scored more touchdowns. Can you figure out how many points each team had, and who won the game?

SCORING RECAP

SAINTS	49ERS
Safety	Touchdown
Touchdown	PAT
PAT	Touchdown
Touchdown	PAT
PAT	Touchdown
Field goal	2-point conversion
Field goal	
Field goal	
TOTAL:	**TOTAL:**

15

The NFL is full of great players. There are bruising running backs such as the Titans' Chris Johnson and the 49ers' Frank Gore. And there are explosive wide receivers such as the Texans' Andre Johnson and the Dolphins' Brandon Marshall. But who is the best? How do you compare them? One way is by using math and examining their statistics.

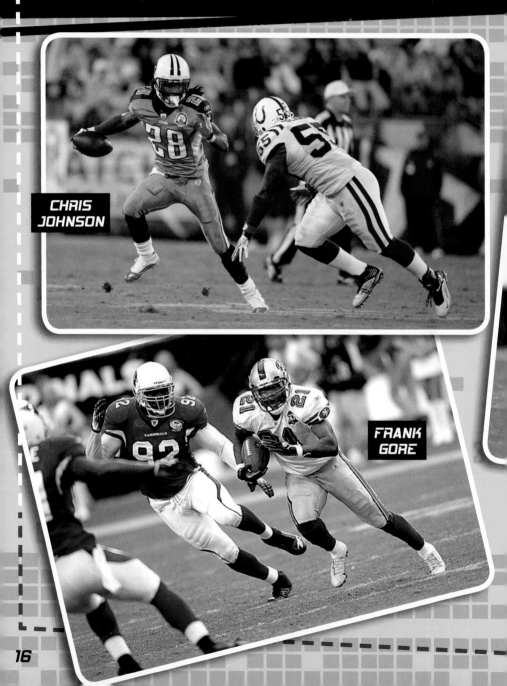

CHRIS
JOHNSON

FRANK
GORE

The best running backs are the workhorses for their teams. They can get 20 or more carries a game in hopes of gaining positive yards each time. A running back's abilities can be measured by their total yards, total touchdowns, yards per attempt, and yards per game.

Figuring out yards per attempt or yards per game means figuring out the average. If a player has a 120-yard rushing day and carried the ball 25 times, how many yards does he gain per attempt?

120 yards / 25 carries = 4.8 yards/carry

ARIAN FOSTER

You can figure out a player's yards per game the same way. Arian Foster of the Houston Texans finished the 2010 season with 1,616 yards and played in all 16 games. Use the same formula for yards per attempt to calculate his yards per game.

1,616 yards / 16 games = 101 yards/game

GOOD HANDS, FAST FEET

Like running backs, wide receivers and tight ends have yards-per-game statistics. But instead of yards per carry, receivers have yards per reception. They are calculated the same way—by finding the average.

For example, Brandon Lloyd of the Denver Broncos had a great 2010 season. He racked up 1,448 yards on 77 receptions in 16 games. How many yards did he gain per game?

$$\frac{1,448 \text{ yards}}{16 \text{ games}} = 90.5 \text{ yards/game}$$

BRANDON LLOYD

Use the same formula to calculate Lloyd's yards per reception.

$$\frac{1,448 \text{ yards}}{77 \text{ receptions}} = 18.8 \text{ yards/reception}$$

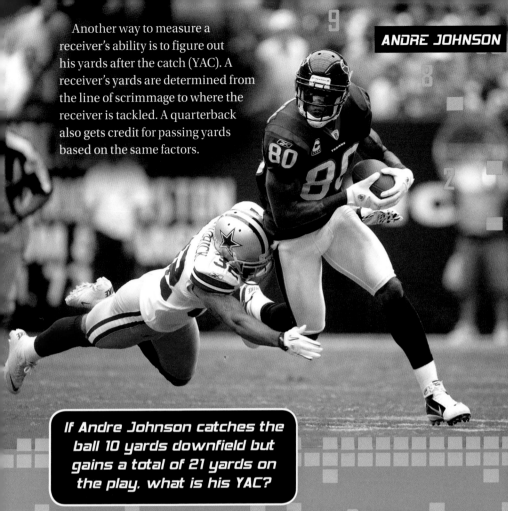

Another way to measure a receiver's ability is to figure out his yards after the catch (YAC). A receiver's yards are determined from the line of scrimmage to where the receiver is tackled. A quarterback also gets credit for passing yards based on the same factors.

If Andre Johnson catches the ball 10 yards downfield but gains a total of 21 yards on the play, what is his YAC?

ANSWER: 11 yards

WES WELKER

The New England Patriots' Wes Welker is one of the NFL's best yards-after-catch receivers. In 2009 he had 1,348 receiving yards, with 709 of those yards coming after he caught the football. That was more than half of his yards. A year earlier Welker had 1,165 yards with 751 coming after the catch.

PLANNING THE ROUTE

When a quarterback takes the snap and drops back to pass, he has several things to think about: Is his offensive line giving him enough time to pass? Is a linebacker blitzing? Is there a safety lurking deep down the field? Are his receivers open? The quarterback has just a few seconds before firing the ball to a receiver. And the throw has to be timed just right.

Meanwhile, receivers have to be precise on their routes. They need to make strong, quick cuts to form angles depending on the play. These quick moves help them separate from the defender.

Pass plays can form triangles on the field. Receivers run routes that make angles with the line of scrimmage or their initial routes. Quarterbacks complete the triangle with their throws.

If the triangle formed is a right triangle, meaning it has a 90-degree angle, you can use the Pythagorean theorem to calculate how far the receiver has to run to make the catch.

$$a^2 + b^2 = c^2$$

The **c** in the equation is the hypotenuse of the triangle.

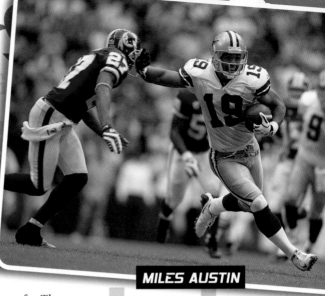

We want to find the distance of **c**. The distance between the quarterback and the wide receiver while they are on the line of scrimmage is **a**. The distance the quarterback throws the ball is **b**. And the distance the wide receiver runs on his route is **c**.

Let's say Dallas Cowboys' wide receiver Miles Austin lines up 10 yards away from quarterback Tony Romo. After the snap Romo throws a bullet to Austin 15 yards downfield. How far did Austin have to run to make the catch?

The distance Austin travels is the hypotenuse of the triangle, so we have to solve for **c**.

$$10^2 + 15^2 = c^2$$
$$c^2 = 100 + 225$$
$$c^2 = 325$$

To solve for **c**, take the square root of both sides of the equation. The square root cancels out the square on the left side, leaving only **c**. That means **c** equals the square root of 325.

$$c = \sqrt{325}$$
$$c = 18 \text{ yards}$$

Austin ran 18 yards from the line of scrimmage to make the catch.

21

PASSING FANCY

Few players get as much attention as quarterbacks. They run the offense, and when it comes time to pass the ball, the games ride on their arms. A quarterback's skills can be measured by several passing statistics, including completion percentage, passing yards, average yards per completion, touchdowns, and touchdown-to-interception ratio.

	TOM BRADY	PEYTON MANNING
GAMES	16	16
COMPLETIONS	324	450
ATTEMPTS	492	679
PASSING YARDS	3,900	4,700
TOUCHDOWNS	36	33
INTERCEPTIONS	4	17

To get a better look at these statistics, let's compare 2010 seasons from two of the best quarterbacks in the NFL: the New England Patriots' Tom Brady and the Indianapolis Colts' Peyton Manning.

TOM BRADY

Let's start with each quarterback's completion percentage. To determine the percentage, divide the number of completions by the number of attempts.

BRADY: 324 / 492 = 65.9%

MANNING: 450 / 679 = 66.3%

Although the numbers are very close, Manning had a better completion percentage by 0.4 percent. How did the quarterbacks compare in passing yards per game?

BRADY:

$$\frac{3,900 \text{ yards}}{16 \text{ games}} = 243.8 \text{ yards/game}$$

MANNING:

$$\frac{4,700 \text{ yards}}{16 \text{ games}} = 293.8 \text{ yards/game}$$

Manning averaged exactly 50 more passing yards per game than Brady. Not to be outdone, Brady scored three more touchdowns than Manning. This is even more impressive when we look at the quarterbacks' touchdown-to-interception ratio. This ratio shows how many touchdowns were scored for every interception thrown.

PEYTON MANNING

BRADY:

$$\frac{36 \text{ touchdowns}}{4 \text{ interceptions}} = 9:1 \text{ ratio}$$

MANNING:

$$\frac{33 \text{ touchdowns}}{17 \text{ interceptions}} = 1.9:1 \text{ ratio}$$

Brady had a much better touchdown-to-interception ratio than Manning. But both quarterbacks had excellent seasons, and each excelled in different areas. That's why it's important to consider all the stats when comparing players.

QUARTERBACK RATING

Another way of measuring a quarterback's performance is by quarterback rating. The rating puts a quarterback's important passing statistics into one formula.

First you need the following quarterback stats: passes completed, passes attempted, passing yards, touchdowns, and interceptions. Then plug the numbers into the following equations.

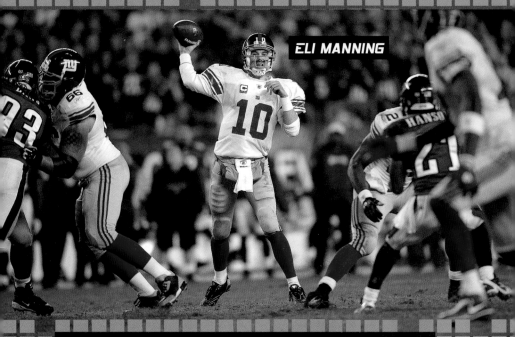

ELI MANNING

A: percentage of completions per attempt
((completions / attempts) − 0.3) * 5

B: average yards gained per attempt
((passing yards / attempts) − 3) / 4

C: percentage of touchdown passes per attempt
(touchdowns / attempts) * 20

D: percentage of interceptions per attempt
2.375 − ((interceptions / attempts) * 25)

RULE: The results of each equation cannot be greater than 2.375 or less than zero. If they are, award 2.375 as a maximum or zero as a minimum.

After you get all of the numbers, you can calculate the quarterback rating using the following equation.

(A + B + C + D) * 100 / 6 = rating

Without numbers it's hard to picture how this all works. Using Chargers' quarterback Philip Rivers' 2010 stats, let's work through the steps.

PHILIP RIVERS' 2010 STATS	
COMPLETIONS	357
ATTEMPTS	541
PASSING YARDS	4,710
TOUCHDOWNS	30
INTERCEPTIONS	13

A: $((357 / 541) - 0.3) * 5 = 1.799$

B: $((4.710 / 541) - 3) / 4 = 1.427$

C: $(30 / 541) * 20 = 1.109$

D: $2.375 - ((13 / 541) * 25) = 1.774$

Then plug the amounts into the following equation.

$$QB\ rating = (A + B + C + D) * 100 / 6$$

$$(1.799 + 1.427 + 1.109 + 1.774) * 100 / 6$$

$$6.109 * 100 / 6$$

$$610.9 / 6$$

Philip Rivers' 2010 QB rating = 101.8

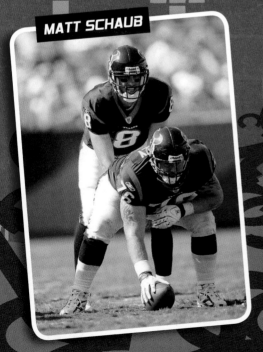

MATT SCHAUB

Can you determine Matt Schaub's QB rating in 2010?	
COMPLETIONS	365
ATTEMPTS	574
PASSING YARDS	4,370
TOUCHDOWNS	24
INTERCEPTIONS	12

ANSWER: 92.0

25

DISTRIBUTING THE BALL

In Super Bowl XLV, Green Bay Packers quarterback Aaron Rodgers completed 24 of 39 passes on his way to a win and MVP honors. Eight different receivers made catches in that game. The chart shows how the passes were distributed.

JORDY NELSON	9
JAMES JONES	5
GREG JENNINGS	4
DONALD DRIVER	2
BRANDON JACKSON	1
ANDREW QUARLESS	1
KOREY HALL	1
TOM CRABTREE	1

AARON RODGERS

To get a better look at Rodgers' pass distribution, we can put the numbers into a pie chart. Pie charts are helpful to see the parts or percentages of a whole.

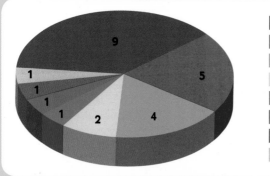

AARON RODGERS' PASS DISTRIBUTION, SUPER BOWL XLV

Jordy Nelson
James Jones
Greg Jennings
Donald Driver
Brandon Jackson
Andrew Quarless
Korey Hall
Tom Crabtree

It's easy to see that Jordy Nelson caught the most passes. You can also get a good estimate of what percentage of the passes Nelson caught. It's less than one half (50 percent), but more than one quarter (25 percent). Let's do the math to figure out the exact percentage.

9 / 24 = 37.5

Nelson caught 37.5 percent of Rodgers' passes.

Ben Roethlisberger had a similar passing game for the Pittsburgh Steelers in Super Bowl XLV. He completed 25 of 40 passes to eight receivers. Take a look at the pie chart and answer the following questions about Roethlisberger's performance.

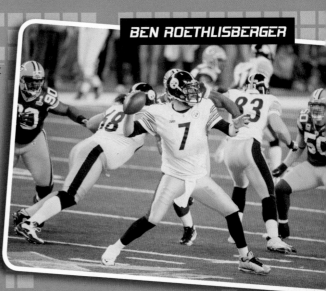

BEN ROETHLISBERGER

BEN ROETHLISBERGER'S PASS DISTRIBUTION, SUPER BOWL XLV

MIKE WALLACE
MATT SPAETH
RASHARD MENDENHALL
ANTONIO BROWN
HINES WARD
ANTWANN RANDLE EL
EMMANUEL SNADERS
HEATH MILLER

2 2 2
7
9
1 1 1

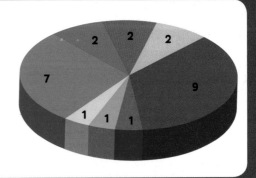

1) Which player had the most catches?

2) The second most?

3) Which three players had the fewest catches?

CHAPTER 3

DEFENSE! DEFENSE!

Although most of the attention in football goes to the offense, many games are decided by the defense. The defensive players work together to stop the offense. That's why many of the defensive stats give credit to teamwork.

JEROD MAYO

What's the main job for a defensive player? Tackle the player who has the ball! If a defensive player tackles someone by himself, he's awarded a solo tackle. If he helps his teammate bring down an opposing player, he gets an assist. To determine a player's total tackles, simply add his assists and solo tackles. For example, Jerod Mayo of the New England Patriots led the NFL in tackles in 2010. He had 113 solo tackles and 61 assists for 174 total tackles.

Which player had the most total tackles in 2010?

PLAYER	SOLO	ASSISTS
JAMES LAURINAITIS	98	16
LONDON FLETCHER	87	49
JAMES ANDERSON	101	29

ANSWER: London Fletcher
(Fletcher, 136; Anderson, 130; Laurinaitis, 114)

The statistic for quarterback sacks works in a similar way. If a player sacks the quarterback by himself, he earns a 1 in the sack column. If he had help bringing the quarterback down, he gets 0.5. That's why you'll often see a number that ends in .5 in that category. In 2010 DeMarcus Ware of the Dallas Cowboys had 16.5 sacks—a little more than one per game!

While defensive linemen work to sack the quarterback, the cornerbacks and safeties are always on the lookout to pick off a pass. When the ball is in the air, they must decide whether they have the angle on the pass to try to knock it away or intercept it. If they time it perfectly, they might pick off the ball and maybe even return it for a touchdown. If they miss, though, they could give up a big play.

ED REED

Interceptions can change a game's momentum, especially if the defensive player can get extra yards or a touchdown. The Baltimore Ravens' Ed Reed led the NFL with eight interceptions in 2010.

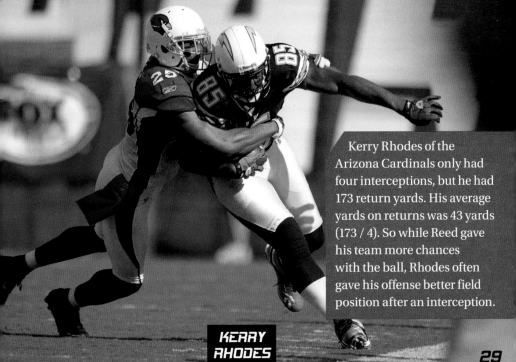

Kerry Rhodes of the Arizona Cardinals only had four interceptions, but he had 173 return yards. His average yards on returns was 43 yards (173 / 4). So while Reed gave his team more chances with the ball, Rhodes often gave his offense better field position after an interception.

KERRY RHODES

GETTING YOUR KICKS

The game is called football, but you don't see feet being used too often. But kickers are important to the game. Many times the outcome of a game rides squarely on their shoes. They have to accurately kick field goals and score points for their team.

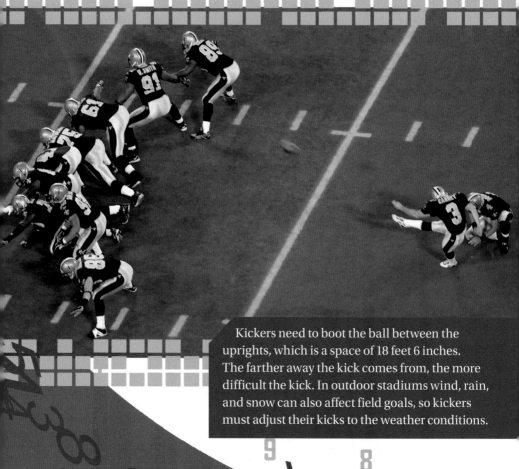

Kickers need to boot the ball between the uprights, which is a space of 18 feet 6 inches. The farther away the kick comes from, the more difficult the kick. In outdoor stadiums wind, rain, and snow can also affect field goals, so kickers must adjust their kicks to the weather conditions.

To measure the distance of a field goal, take the yard line the ball is on and add 10 yards for the end zone. Then add another seven yards to the spot where the ball is being held for the kicker. If a team's drive stalls on the 32-yard line and the coach decides to kick a field goal, how long will the attempted field goal be?

ANSWER: 32 + 10 + 7 = 49 yards

To kick the ball as far as they can, kickers want to send the ball on a 45-degree trajectory. But it's not just about being able to kick the ball a long way. They may want to kick the ball with a higher trajectory so it gets over the defensive players' hands. However, with a higher trajectory, the ball won't go as far. If a kicker is facing a long field goal, he will have to use a lower trajectory so the ball will travel farther. That means it will be easier for the defense to get the block.

JASON ELAM

The longest field goal in NFL history was 63 yards. Two players have accomplished the feat: the Saints' Tom Dempsey in 1970 and the Broncos' Jason Elam in 1998.

GETTING A LEG UP

When a team faces fourth down and is too far away to kick a field goal, it will usually punt the ball. The hope is that the punter will kick the ball far enough away and give it enough hang time so the opponent will have poor field position. In order to do that, the punter should try to kick the ball at a 45-degree angle. Similar to kicking field goals, if a punter uses a 45-degree trajectory, the ball will have the perfect balance between hang time and distance. But that's not always the approach punters want to take.

A larger angle will put the ball higher in the air but might not allow it to travel as far. For example, a 90-degree angle would give the ball an amazing hang time, but it would go straight above the punter' head. A lower angle might make the ball go farther. But the short hang time won't allow the punter's teammates to get down field and tackle the punt returner for a short gain. Plus, an oncoming defender would likely block a football kicked at a 20-degree angle.

What happens after the punt is just as important to a punter. A touchback? No return? A return for a touchdown? Any of those things could happen, which is why one of the most important punting statistics is not gross yards, but net yards.

gross yards: the total yards the ball is kicked

net yards: the total yards gained or lost on the kick after the return

DEVIN HESTER

Here are two punt plays that end up with similar results.

Punting from his team's own 30-yard line, the Titans' Brett Kern booms a 60-yard punt. But the Bears' Devin Hester returns the punt 20 yards, going from his own 10 to the 30-yard line. What is the gross? What is the net?

ANSWER: gross: 60 yards; net: 40 yards

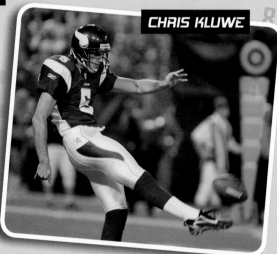

CHRIS KLUWE

The Vikings' Chris Kluwe also punts from the 30-yard line, but the ball only travels 40 yards to the other 30-yard line. However, his gunners get down the field and tackle the Browns' Josh Cribbs for a 3-yard loss. The ball ends up on the 27. What is the gross? What is the net?

ANSWER: gross: 40 yards; net: 43 yards

The longest punt in NFL history was 98 yards. The Jets' Steve O'Neal set the record in 1969 when his team had to punt from its own 1-yard line. O'Neal kicked it out of the back of his own end zone. The ball traveled 75 yards in the air and it bounced and rolled to the Broncos' 1-yard line.

☐ APPLYING THE MATH

PREDICTING THE FUTURE

A few weeks into the season, you can try to predict what players are going to do over the entire season. For instance, if a running back rushes for 100 yards in each of his first three games, you can use math to estimate how many rushing yards he'll have at the end of the season. A simple formula called cross multiplication is used to make your prediction.

TOM BRADY

Let's take Tom Brady's 50-touchdown season of 2007 as an example. No quarterback had ever reached 50 touchdown passes in a season before. But through three games, people began to think about the possibility. They compared Brady's 10 touchdowns over three games to an unknown number over a full 16-game schedule.

$$\frac{10}{3} = \frac{x}{16}$$

10 / 3 = x / 16

34

Using cross multiplication, solve for x.

$$10 * 16 = 3 * x$$
$$160 = 3x$$

Divide both sides by 3 to leave x by itself.

$$160 / 3 = x$$
$$x = 53.3$$

Round that number down, and you could have predicted that Tom Brady would throw 53 touchdown passes that season—pretty close!

CLAY MATTHEWS

Sometimes the predictions don't come true. A player might heat up halfway through the season, or he might start strong and cool off after a few games. In 2010 Green Bay Packers' linebacker Clay Matthews had six sacks after the first two games. At that pace, how many sacks would he have at the end of the season?

$$\frac{6}{2} = \frac{x}{16}$$
$$6 * 16 = 2 * x$$
$$96 = 2x$$
$$96 / 2 = x$$
$$x = 48$$

Forty-eight sacks would have crushed the all-time, single-season sack record of 22.5, but Matthews didn't keep up that incredible pace. After four games he had seven sacks, which still would have put him on pace for a 28-sack season. He ended up finishing the season with 13.5 sacks in 15 games.

MEAN, MEDIAN, MODE, AND RANGE

Looking at a player's averages is a good way to measure his value. But there are other ways of breaking down those numbers over time. We can look at a player's stats in a different way by figuring out the mean (average), median, mode, and range. In 2010 the Atlanta Falcons' Roddy White led the NFL with 115 receptions. Look at White's catches week by week.

RODDY WHITE

WEEK 1	13
WEEK 2	7
WEEK 3	5
WEEK 4	7
WEEK 5	5
WEEK 6	6
WEEK 7	11
WEEK 8	4
WEEK 9	12
WEEK 10	9
WEEK 11	5
WEEK 12	7
WEEK 13	8
WEEK 14	7
WEEK 15	3
WEEK 16	6

We already know how to calculate his mean receptions per game (115 / 16 = 7.2). But what about the median, mode, and range?

To find the median, mode, and range, organize White's numbers from lowest to highest.

3 4 5 5 5 6 6 7 7 7 7 8 9 11 12 13

mean—the average amount of a set of numbers

median—the middle number in a list of numbers

mode—the number in a list that is repeated most often

range—the difference between the largest and smallest value

There is an even amount of numbers in the list. So to find the median, take the average of the two middle numbers. Both middle numbers are 7, so the median is 7.

Next let's find the mode. White had seven catches in a game four times, while he had five catches only three times. So the mode is 7.

To calculate the range, simply subtract the lowest number from the highest number (13 – 3). The range is 10.

Notice that White's numbers are all similar. That means he was mostly consistent over the entire season.

BRANDON MARSHALL

In 2009 the Broncos' Brandon Marshall set the NFL record for catches in a single game with 21 receptions. How did this affect his mean, median, mode, and range?

Marshall's receptions over 15 games: 3 3 4 4 4 5 5 5 6 7 7 8 8 11 21

What was Marshall's mean, median, mode, and range? (Hint: There are two answers for mode).

ANSWER: mean: 6.7; median: 5; mode: 4 and 5; range: 18

Marshall had a great 2009 season with 101 receptions, but he was not as consistent as White was in 2010.

TURNOVERS AND RATIOS

Turnovers drive players, coaches, and fans crazy. Colts fans cringed when the Saints' Tracy Porter intercepted Peyton Manning's pass late in Super Bowl XLIV and returned it for a touchdown. Fortunately for the Colts, Manning doesn't cough up the ball much.

Turnovers are a big part of the game, which is why turnover stats are important. Look at how often a running back fumbles or the rate in which a quarterback throws an interception. You can see how much of a liability they are when they have the ball.

TRACY PORTER

In 2009 Adrian Peterson of the Minnesota Vikings developed a reputation for fumbling the ball. He lost six fumbles that season, while touching the ball (rushing and receiving) 357 times. How often did he lose the ball?

$$357 / 6 = 59.5$$

That stat means he turned over the ball once every 60 times he was given the ball. Peterson got better, though. In 2010 he lost only one fumble on 319 touches.

DREW BREES

During the 2010 season, Drew Brees of the New Orleans Saints completed 448 of 658 passes with 33 touchdowns and 22 interceptions. To calculate how often Brees threw an interception, divide the number of passes attempted by the number of interceptions.

658 / 22 = 29.9

Brees threw an interception for every 30 passes he attempted. Let's compare that with the Jacksonville Jaguars' David Garrard. He threw 15 interceptions in 2010, but he only had 366 attempts. How many passes per interception did Garrard have in 2010?

Answer: 24.4 (366 / 15)

DAVID GARRARD

ROUGH AND TOUGH

Football is one of the grittiest, hardest-hitting contact sports. The bone-crunching hits and powerful tackles can shake up the best players. Let's see how math plays into the action.

While football players are moving on the field, they have momentum. A player's momentum is calculated using his mass and velocity.

$$momentum = mass * velocity$$

Let's say Buffalo Bills wide receiver Stevie Johnson is running a route straight down the field. Cornerback Charles Tillman of the Chicago Bears is running in stride with him. Because both players are moving at the same velocity, the player with more mass will also have more momentum. Momentum is measured in kilogram-meters per second.

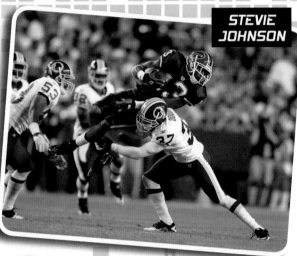

STEVIE JOHNSON

CHARLES TILLMAN

JOHNSON:
momentum =
92 kg * 5 m/second

momentum =
460 kg-m/second

TILLMAN:
momentum =
90 kg * 5 m/second

momentum =
450 kg-m/second

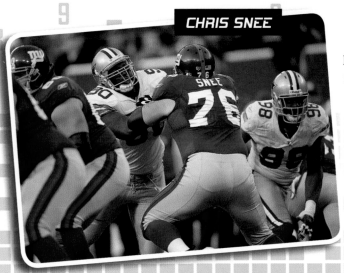

CHRIS SNEE

A player's momentum has a big impact on the force of a hit. During a hit, kinetic energy—the energy of motion—is transferred from one player to another. Kinetic energy is measured in joules.

$$kinetic\ energy = \tfrac{1}{2}\ mass * velocity^2$$

Who would have more kinetic energy—offensive lineman Chris Snee of the New York Giants or Jared Allen of the Minnesota Vikings? Snee has more mass, but it's likely that Allen is moving at a greater velocity. If Snee is trying to block Allen, he is probably only moving about 1 meter/second. If Allen gets a good jump on the snap, he might be moving at 2 meters/second when he comes into contact with Snee. Given each player's mass, can you determine which player has more kinetic energy?

JARED ALLEN

SNEE:
mass = 144 kg
velocity = 1 m/second

ALLEN:
mass = 122 kg
velocity = 2 m/second

Answer: Jared Allen
(Allen's KE = 244 joules; Snee's KE = 72 joules)

Football has been around for a long time, but it hasn't always been played the same. Over time teams have changed their strategies and started new trends. For example, football was much more of a running game in the early 1920s. Passing was rare. To get a better picture of the upward trend, we can use a line graph to chart each season's leading quarterback in passing yards per game.

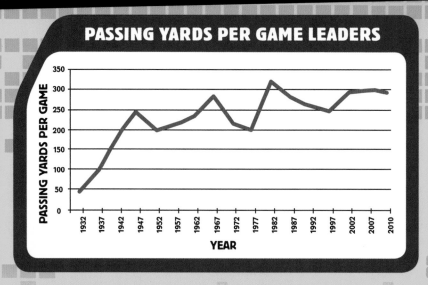

PASSING YARDS PER GAME LEADERS

Looking at the graph, it's easy to see that the emphasis on passing has gone up since the early 1930s. The top quarterback in 1932, Green Bay's Arnie Herber, threw for only 45.6 yards per game. Fifty years later San Diego's Dan Fouts passed for more than seven times that number each game.

Each year it seems professional football players are bigger, faster, and stronger. But how much bigger are players getting? Using a bar graph, let's take a look at how many 300-pound athletes have played in the NFL. In 1970 there was one. In 2009 there were almost 400.

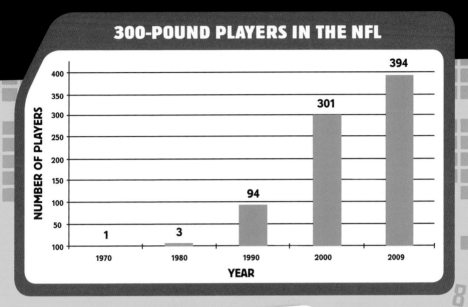

300-POUND PLAYERS IN THE NFL

NUMBER OF PLAYERS

Year	1970	1980	1990	2000	2009
	1	3	94	301	394

YEAR

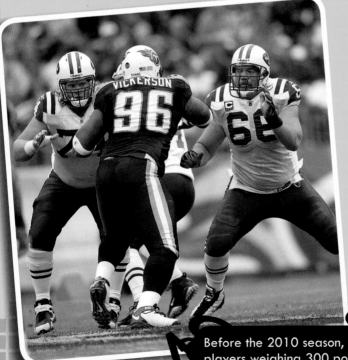

VICKERSON 96

62

The bar graph shows how much of an increase there has been in the number of 300-pound players in the NFL. Between which two decades did the number of 300-pound players increase the most?

Answer: 1990 and 2000

Before the 2010 season, at least 500 players weighing 300 pounds or more took part in NFL training camps.

In 2010 the New England Patriots had the league's best regular-season record, 14–2. The Patriots were also the NFL's top-scoring team, racking up 518 points. Meanwhile, the Carolina Panthers had the opposite record, 2–14. The Panthers were the NFL's lowest-scoring team with only 196 points.

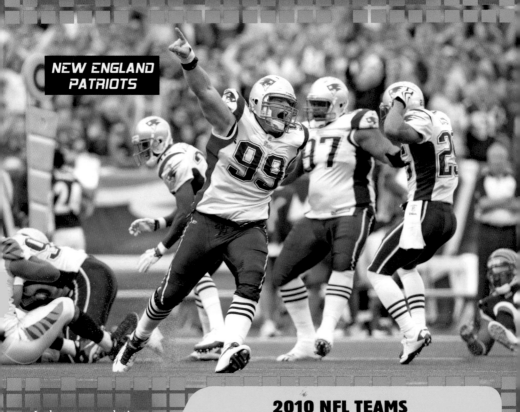

NEW ENGLAND PATRIOTS

Is there a correlation between the number of points scored and a team's record? One way to find out is by using a graph called a scatter plot that allows you to track statistics. In this case you can plot a team's points and wins on a graph. After filling in all 32 NFL teams, here's what the scatter plot looks like:

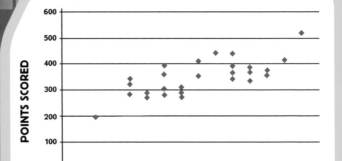

2010 NFL TEAMS

(scatter plot: x-axis "WINS" from 0 to 15; y-axis "POINTS SCORED" from 0 to 600)

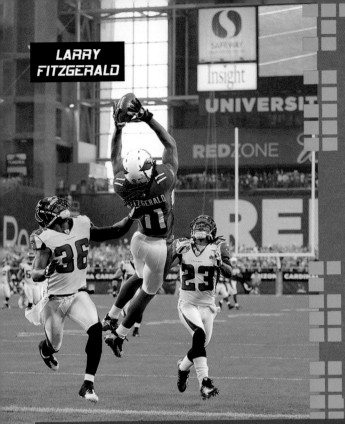

LARRY FITZGERALD

Sure enough, the point totals (y axis) tend to rise as the win totals (x axis) increase. If you draw a diagonal line through the middle of the dots, there will be an equal number of plots above and below the line. This is called a positive correlation. The line—called the line of best fit—can also be used to predict results. For instance, six teams had 10 wins, and their point totals ranged from 341 to 439. The line of best fit puts a 10-win team around 400 points.

Sometimes there is no correlation between two statistics. Take a look at a scatter plot that marks the receptions and touchdowns for the top receivers in 2010:

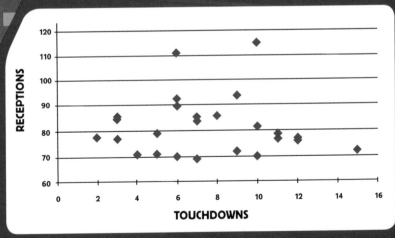

2010 RECEIVERS

RECEPTIONS (y axis): 60, 70, 80, 90, 100, 110, 120

TOUCHDOWNS (x axis): 0, 2, 4, 6, 8, 10, 12, 14, 16

The plots on the graph are all over—they don't resemble a line. That means there isn't a strong correlation between receptions and touchdowns. Just because a receiver has a lot of receptions, it doesn't mean he will score more touchdowns.

GLOSSARY

area—the amount of surface within a specific boundary; area is measured in square units

kinetic energy—the energy of motion

mass—the amount of matter in an object

mean—the average amount of a set of numbers

median—the middle number in a list of numbers

mode—the number in a list that is repeated the most often

momentum—a property of a moving object equal to its mass times its velocity

Pythagorean theorem—an equation used to find the third side of a right triangle ($a^2 + b^2 = c^2$)

range—the difference between the largest and smallest value in a list of numbers

ratio—a comparison of two quantities expressed in numbers

route—the path a receiver follows during a play

time of possession (TOP)—the amount of time a team has control of the ball

velocity—a measurement of both the speed and direction an object is moving

wild card—a team that doesn't win its division but still has a good enough record to make the playoffs

yards after catch (YAC)—a statistic used to measure the number of yards a receiver gains after catching the ball

READ MORE

Biskup, Agnieszka. *Football: How it Works.* The Science of Sports. Mankato, Minn.: Capstone Press, 2010.

Mahaney, Ian F. *The Math of Football.* Sports Math. New York: PowerKids Press, 2011.

Marsico, Katie, and Cecilia Minden. *Football.* Real World Math: Sports. Ann Arbor, Mich.: Cherry Lake Pub., 2009.

INTERNET SITES

FactHound offers a safe, fun way to find Internet sites related to this book. All of the sites on FactHound have been researched by our staff.

Here's all you do:

Visit *www.facthound.com*

Type in this code: 9781429665674

Super-cool stuff!

Check out projects, games and lots more at
www.capstonekids.com

INDEX